# ORDINARY MAGIC
# And Other Ceremonies

by Gwenana

La Jolla Poets Press
P.O. Box 8638
La Jolla, CA 92038

## ABOUT THE ILLUSTRATOR

*Jedd Strange, a graduate of the California Institute of the Arts, 1977, is a freelance artist. His work appears in all three books of a trilogy by Gwenana, as well as books for other authors. Not only an illustrator and book designer, Jedd is a distinguished muralist whose work graces many Southern California walls. As a member of the Screen Cartoonist Guild he has worked widely as an animator.*

*Gwenana says of Jedd: "The artist embraced my manuscript to find its pulse as though it were a living creature. Then, to that beat, creative images emerged and gave my words another form."*

## EDITOR: JONNIE TAYLOR-LEIDT

Carlsbad, CA

## COVER & ILLUSTRATIONS: JEDD STRANGE

San Diego, CA

## COPYRIGHT 1987 BY GWENDOLYN A. JANSMA

ISBN: 0-931721-06-7
'Library of Congress Catalog Number:' 87-83379

## PUBLISHER: KATHLEEN IDDINGS

La Jolla Poets Press
P.O. Box 8638
La Jolla, CA 92038

# Trilogy of Poems

## by
## Gwenana

**THE BLESSED ORDINARY**
Wounds and Healings

**ORDINARY WISDOM**
and Other Treasures

**ORDINARY MAGIC**
and Other Ceremonies

# FOREWORD:
## Poetry as Celebration of Adventure

Poetry is a celebration of wonder joined to a desire to share with others. Why else do prophets speak to others of revelations given directly to the heart? To bridge the chasm separating hearts and to communicate with others Gwenana resorts to images made of words. She remembers wonder and passes on its beauty to others, inviting her readers to enjoy her heart's vision, maybe even to learn.

Poets are philosophers, especially today when academic practitioners of this art nitpick over conundrums long rendered dry bones by years spent alone. Sometimes we need to learn philosophy anew from poets.

This poet's philosophy comes from experience and reflection. These capsules of Gwenana's contain fragrances and essences of treasured adventures. We read the poet's heart opened to us so we may adventure together.

Hers is a visionary poetry which takes our hand in common language made elegant by verse. Words may hold many secrets as if forever to conceal what they bravely try to reveal. Used by poets these same words with sweet freshness, delicately reveal things unrecognized.

She records reflections on childhood, mothering, and on her own growth in the transcendence of trance and spiritual inner adventuring. In ancient poetic garb appropriate to her subject, Gwenana recreates for us her shamano-mysticism.

She remains faithful to her muse's ideal throughout; that animating genius we have all sought, now shared openly and abundantly with us.

Prof. Willard Johnson
Vista, California
Fall, 1987

# AUTHOR'S NOTE

Long ago, when the world was new to me, magic was anything my unfolding mind could not yet grasp nor hands perform. As a child I found magic everywhere Gradually, however, the diamonds turned to dewdrops and wonder began to live in the corners of my life rather than at the center.

The black or white world presented to me by my traditional family, cultural religion, and traditional schools provided the timber from which I began to construct boxes for my thinking and experiencing. I also began collecting excuses and explanations for my many magical shadings of gray. Mother provided phrases such as 'it's just a dream' and 'it's only your imagination.' My church gave me 'hocus-pocus' and 'the devil's work.' From friends I gathered 'quirks,' and 'weirdness;' from school, 'coincidence.' Advanced education gifted me with 'neurotic,' and even worse, 'psychotic.'

Yet, my curious fingers found buttons and a voice deep within would say 'push,' and lids flew open and my eyes grew wide and my mind and heart expanded and slowly magic returned to inspire me.

Then I began to search for all the shadings of life, to explore the unusual and different, to bring the extraordinary into my ordinary world, to open myself and embrace all of my experience without judgment or disparagement.

The poems in this book were written from that expansion and that embrace.

Perhaps you will find familiar territory here. Perhaps you will need to stand on tiptoe, stretch your beliefs, find cracks in your own boxes to experience a lightening that leads to joy. You may even be taken by surprise to hear an echo coming from deep within and you, too, may call it magic.

To enhance our sense of connection I have placed footnotes throughout this book to serve as stepping stones, small places where we may briefly stand together and adjust our eyes for the magic ahead.

## DEDICATION

To all who journey with me
toward that larger world of wonder
most often found in childhood.

## I Would

If I could gently touch
    your eye of doubt
    and help you raise the lid
    to sights now hidden,
If I could wrap my arms
    around your heart
    so fearful of the seeing,
If I could help you trust that universe
    around the edges of your ordinary senses
    and see the main event,
I would.

I would.

(1) footnote

*Everyone's life has its turning points, moments of opening, and flashes of illumination. I have tried to gather the flavors of the ordinary turnings of life, hoping you will taste again some of your own awakening moments, graduations, small deaths, or the wedding of yourself to a new reality or to the same person in a new way. Perhaps you will also feel again the yearnings that call to the unfoldings and celebrate with me the magic of the journey.*

## Childhood

*Spring-tender shoot was I*
*as I split open,*
*with fragile edge,*
*the wintered earth.*

*I had to suck so hard*
*on all that barren land*
*to find a little nourishment*
*for soul.*

## Free-Floating Fear

A dance of demons flickers
     just beyond my fingertips.
I force my eyes to look
     on safer paths
     and breathe in carefully,
     afraid of sucking in the dust
     from dancing feet.

The stillness of this refuge place
     prevents the freedom winds
     from catching in my hair
     and lifting me
     beyond the dance.

## Questions

*What is this whistling through my ears?*
*It sounds like fear,*
   *the fear of knowing the unknown.*

*Who is this telling shamans what to do?*
*It feels like me, the Me of me,*
   *the One I dare not be.*

## My Path

Some people ask me how I find my path,
    assume perhaps,
    I find it in some book
    or Thomas Brothers map.
That's not the way it is.

It's more like driving in the fog
    and seeing just enough
    to slowly move ahead
    trusting the road continues
    to a far-off hidden place
    where Someone lights the lamps of home.

## Life History

I took a hook of innocence
    and swung it 'round my head
    and I went 'round and 'round,
    a heady spin,
    going nowhere.

I took a hand, an offered hand, in mine
    and twined our fingers tight.
Then we touched spots unfelt before.
A soft wind blew,
    the wind of lifting veils.

Again, I took that hook of innocence
    and swung it 'round my head.
I tore the veils,
    my flesh,
    my life,
    and I fell down.

I took another offered hand.
This time I let the love run free enough
    to gully through my fears,
    to tear up roots.

Then finally,
I took my Self,
    my broken, mended, bleeding,
    healing, humbled, holy Self,
    and made a hook of me.
I stretched,
    and just beyond my fingertips was Soul.
I felt the warmth that leads to fire
    and drew back.
Yet, drawn to fire that felt like death
    and stretching more,
    I touched my Soul
    and grabbed it by the throat.

*The needle's eye loomed small.*
*I trembled at the task,*
    *and trembling shook me loose of Self*
    *but not of Soul.*
*Then Soul hung onto Self and pulled*
    *and with this energy*
    *released whatever keeps my Soul inside,*
    *and I turned inside out.*

## Yearnings

*Tonight,*
*I look into my lover's eyes*
  *and see the void in us,*
    *reflection of the void in my own soul.*
*These are the hollows made by yearnings—*
    *for God, for union,*
      *nameless one?*
*I do not know.*

*I only know*
    *these yearnings make my eyes bleed tears*
    *and scoop my body pulp.*
*These yearnings cramp my heart*
    *and from their nest push genitals.*

*On the river of these yearnings*
    *I could drift into death,*
    *could swim with Atlas-arms into death,*
    *and welcome it.*

## My Awakening

*Inside somewhere*
*a bubble burst.*
*A tender membrane split*
*releasing me*
*to soar beyond my reach,*
*to give each cell a space and time*
*of different quality.*

*Now I am free*
*to welcome all the sounds*
*that play between the notes,*
*to keep the treasures*
*of my lifetime gatherings,*
*and finally,*
*to find my self-soul's natural music.*

## First Light

I feel the dawn
  that's breaking in my heart.
First light creeps in
  along the pathway
  to my inner sleeping self.

Champagning bursts of happiness
  lift locks of apathy
  and roll away the pebbles
  from my eyes.

I see.

I sing.

I am.

### It's Me!

Perhaps you've seen the ribbons
flying in the sky,
and thought you saw a rainbow
or a river lost from gravity?

Oh, no,
you see,
it's me you see.
It's me!
I'm sending energy,
a stream of healing lavender,
a rosy shade of love,
a streak of gold for purity,
a band of green for growth.

So do look out,
and up,
and pull one in
and thread it through your heart.
I'll feel the gentle tug,
and know,
you see it's me!

## A Color of My Soul

*Oh, pieces of my soul*
*that take the form of azure,*
*sometimes I see you gathering*
*with other azure souls*
*to sing the surface of the ocean into being,*
*or, playfully,*
*leave fingerprints in tidepools.*

*Oh, azure pieces of my soul,*
*you move the mighty rivers of the world,*
*give substance*
*to the vastness in between the stars,*
*yet also take the lower road*
*to ride inside a single tear*
*that slowly finds its way to earth.*

## Wedding Day

*I always thought*
*that phoenix birds and resurrections*
*were things that happened long ago*
*and far away.*

*I never thought*
*that I'd be brushing ashes from my sleeve.*
*I never thought*
*my arms would hold the sun,*
*or that the bells of earth*
*would ring for me.*

*I hear you speak of soulmate,*
*lover, friend,*
*and rhapsodize*
*on mergings, marriage, matings.*
*I only know*
*my eyes are wet with golden tears,*
*my grays of life are rainbows, now.*

*For fire burned through*
*my walls of guilt and willfulness,*
*and left me vulnerable to love.*
*And I, for once,*
*did not resist the flame.*

*Ahh, phoenix birds and resurrections*
*can happen here and now to me and you*
*and all who dare*
*to brave the fires of love.*

### In My Life Are Three Deaths

One morning
  I woke up and realized
  I was dead.

My death resulted
  from the very acts
  that promise life—
  the rituals of mating,
  merging, procreating.

For some,
  these acts that deadened me,
  enliven.
Perhaps they are the ones
  who hold the reins
  and know their best direction.
I didn't.

My best direction seemed like a river
  underground, long buried,
  preceding me in death.

My reins were placed
  in other hands
  and I went for the ride—
  the winds of which cemented me
  into a form that killed.

But fortunately,
  one morning I woke up
  and realized I was dead.

The second time I died
  I held the reins.
Deliberately, I held the knife
  and did the cutting
  of my fears, my doubts.
I bled.

And in the letting of that blood
  my jugular smelled placenta.
The thrust that split my life
  also revealed my core.
And as I rode the pain
  I saw the wonder of this death
  was life.
For if a death is deep enough
  and traveled all the way,
  then birth rides in its arms.

The third time that I die
  I'll send out invitations
  to a farewell party.
I'll celebrate my births
  and deaths
  with all my fellow travelers.

Then, full of life,
  and on a day that's good for dying,
  I'll very slowly,
  gently,
  pull the curtain down.

And mail a postcard from the other side.

## Pathfinder

Among the names that I've been given
   is one I treasure,
   but sometimes question.

The Namer says that I've been seen
   out kicking in the underbrush
   of women's tethers
   in search of hidden paths
   where only half a footprint
   points direction.

This Namer also says
   I have been caught flat-handed
   sweeping walls of man-made rules
   to find a crack for fingerholds.

She says she knows, first hand,
   that I've impaled myself on thorns
   to blunt the sting for others—
   have saved my tears as talismans
   to help me hold those other salty hands.

I will admit
   that I've been soaring over worlds of worlds
   to find the worms of wisdom.
It seems to me,
   I only try to find my way—
   and yet,
   from time to time,
   I hear some footsteps coming up behind.

## Graduation Message

I came here
  looking for a place to breathe,
  expand the lungs lodged in my mind,
  my heart,
  my spirit, and my body.

I came to breathe
  into the nostrils of the teachers,
  and the searchers,
  and the other wanderers.

And here I found,
  in different ways, a place to breathe,
  and so carved out a way
  of gathering the nourishment I'd looked for
  in so many places, people, things,
  and now discover in myself.

And all the ways I've found
  to be more of myself—
  my thickening of roots and branches
  signifying growth;
  the fires I've been through
  to find myself—
  all this I carry on my breath
  like runners carry flame.

Breathe deeply
  as I send it out into the universe.
It is the breath of transformation.

### The I Am

*Enspirited traditions*
*of the people of this earth empower me.*
*But none is mine for only I am mine.*

## Soul Center

*I finally found
the center of a gyroscope
which is the center
of the universe of me,
the place where all my passions unify
by balancing each other.*

*It is a place of simple truth,
liquidity of all by boundedness.*

*It is the place where every part of God,
revealed in human form,
is touched
but none controls:
the place of inner harmony.*

*I finally found the center of the universe of me
and also found the key for getting there.
Come, take my hand.
The journey to the center of your universe
is long.*

*(2) footnote*

*Perhaps because we are given only brief glimpses, or because they occur in sleep; perhaps because we encounter laughter or ridicule when we speak of them, we paste disowning labels on some of our experiences and file them away from the world. In doing so, we lose sight of a valuable part of ourselves. With the poems that follow I invite you to look through your files for wonders long unattended.*

*(2a) footnote*

*My teachers seem to come around at night and use their magic wands to tap me on the shoulder. In sparks of light created by the tappings I often find my lessons in my dreams.*

## Ordinary Miracles

*Each night*
    *an ordinary miracle occurs.*
*Each night*
    *a different one—*
    *though some repeat.*

*Last night*
    *this miracle was mine:*
*In dream I walked into an ordinary elevator*
    *and pushed a button*
    *for the highest floor.*
*The elevator rose,*
    *the building fell away,*
    *and I continued through the clouds*
    *toward thinning universe.*
*And I could see it all*
    *with eyes that saw through walls.*

*And every night*
    *an ordinary miracle occurs.*

## Common Dilemma

*I dreamed I held a baby*
     *born before his time,*
     *the body soft and warm,*
     *but from the neck grew head*
     *of balding bird.*
*And from this infant's throat*
     *came words that pierced*
     *into the core of truth.*

*The women with me in the dream*
     *were unaware of the deformity*
     *and of the spoken words.*

*In dream, as in my waking world,*
     *I pondered a dilemma—*
     *should I leave ignorance alone,*
     *help others to avoid the pain of looking,*
     *but miss the words that feed their souls?*

## Dream Therapy

*Last night, in dream,*
*the playful part of me*
*tied strips of cloth together*
*and sent this creature*
*to another room which sheltered*
*the obsessive part of me,*
*who promptly breathed these strips*
*into a snake*
*and soon engaged this thing*
*in battle.*
*The sound effects*
*had the intensity of the obsessed*
*combined with playful histrionics.*

*Then silence fell,*
*and I emerged wrapped like a snake*
*wearing a Cheshire grin;*
*and well I might,*
*because obsessive me and playful me,*
*in dream at least,*
*had tamed each other.*

## Shadow of a Doubt

I dreamed the kind of dream
  that comes to haunt me when I waken.
It opens something that's been sealed,
  presents to me a key
  encircled by a dream.

I dreamed I saw two animals
  the shape of snakes
  with heads and fur like foxes.
These animals were being used like rags
  to stuff some leaky ceiling holes.

And all the people in the dream
  believed these foxy snakes were rags.

I saw the evidence of life,
  of heads,
  and tongues and tails.
I called out my reality to deafened ears.
I held out bones and bits of fur
  left from the rats
  these foxy snakes had eaten,
  but these were scoffed out of my hands
  and trampled.

And all the people in the dream
  believed the snakes were rags.

I stood alone.
There were so many more of them.
They looked so wise.
They stood so firm.

My eyes bounced off our two realities
  as waves and waves of wavering
  awakened me.

The haunt of dream is haunt of life
  whenever doubting shakes my inner knowledge.

## The Golden Mean

Last night a woman came to me.
She knelt beside my bed
    inviting me to dance with her.
Then, in a dream, revealed to me
    the steps I'd need
    to dance this dance of mystery.

She helped me lift myself above myself,
    to balance in the sky
    while lying on the ground,
    reflect myself in clouds,
    leave footprints on the earth.

I felt the rocks pressed in my spine,
    a triangle of stars
    pulled at my shoulders,
    and suddenly, I knew:
The dance I'd been invited to
    takes place in balanced energy
    that arcs the universe.
It moves from fingertip to fingertip
    and toe to toe.

## Melody of Life

The language of the dream I dreamed last night
was one of feelings,
a universal language
which often echoes through my day
long after dream's forgotten.

Although there were some pictures in the dream,
they faded in the swelling melody of feelings,
as though my viscera
were rounded pipes belonging to an organ
played by the gentlest of hands.
And even chords of pain
were played in harmony with notes of love.

At times today,
this melody welled up,
discordant with the happenings of waking life,
like tappings on my shoulder,
or someone tugging at my sleeve.

I think the melody
called out a truth I knew but didn't remember—
some feelings may seem like
a mighty, swelling, stops-out organ
when kept inside,
but when let out, accompanied by grace notes,
they form a melody to live by.

## Unfolding in Dream

In dream I twinned,
   then twinned the dream.
And in both dreams
   my heart grew hands
   newly withdrawn from giving birth.

In dream
   these hands pulled lapis stones
   out of my womb
   to form a bench
   that bridged another
   far-off, ancient bench
   seen through the mists
   of other lives.

Next night
   my womb became a silver pool
   reflecting to my mirrored self
   upon the shore
   a box,
   the color of the sky at dawn
   and open to the heavens.

A bench that is a bridge.
A box that's open to the eye of God.
The blueprint of my soul?

*(2b) footnote*

*My intuition lives somewhere inside, much like the elves live in the gingko trees, to gather up reality not often seen in sunlight. So, too, the forest of my ordinary consciousness holds many wonders in its shadowy depths that surface only when my mind is stilled and I call out through prayer or drums or flute or meditation.*

## Beyond My Conscious World

I see the world of my sub-conscious self
    as through a glass, darkly.
It has a quality of time not felt,
    slowed down,
    observed,
    but not experienced as time.

I have a sense of hoverings
    beyond my seeing, touching, hearing;
    the straining sense of knowing
    there is essense out of reach
    that plays around my fingertips.

I have a feeling of surroundedness
    while being the surrounder,
    like symbol of the yin and yang.

When will the clearing come?
When face to face?

## Telephone Encounter

The voice walking the highwire
  to my ear
  was shed of body
  I had never seen.

Yet, in that voice
  I saw pink ballerina shoes
  acquainted with the dance of life.
I heard the cheers
  that welcome first place runners,
  and felt the rush of air
  from scrolls unrolling wisdom
  gathered from her wanderings.

I smelled the wit
  that clears out passages.
I rolled the gift of her
  across my tongue
  and tasted friendship in the making.

## Unconditional Positive Regard

How can I draw a picture
        of the purpose of my life
        that comes from my subconscious mind?

I'll take some crayons and stand beside myself
        to view an absolutely fascinating creature
        as though she were a stranger.
I'll watch
        with all of my attention on her creation,
        and without question, let her have her way.
She'll need no guidance,
        can do no wrong,
        for in that moment
        she will be my precious deeper self.

This drawing will portray my purpose perfectly,
        and seen through eyes of love
        will be quite easily deciphered—
        but equally obscured if judged or analyzed.

## In Prayer or Meditation

*From core of light*
        *residing in the core of me*
*A flow goes out*
*And out*
        *until it fills the universe*
        *with particles*
        *much smaller than a mustard seed*
        *or speck of dust*
        *each colored in full spectrum.*

*These particles then draw me out*
        *until I draw them in again,*
*And as they merge*
        *produce some hues of purest light*
        *red*
        *orange and yellow*
        *green*
        *blue and violet*
        *each focused on a place inside.*
*Then pouring forth while staying in*
        *these particles increase intensity*
        *and fuse into a line*
        *of clearest crystal.*

## Rebirth

In trance that's actively induced
    in hypnotherapy
I take the elevator down to womb
    and there experience a sense of safety,
    of being wrapped around by presence,
    a sense of oneness,
    union.

I seem to know what's going on,
    but not as nine-month fetus
    waiting to be born;
    instead, as aged knowingness
    with life or death attachment
    to the body floating in my mother's womb.

Then, all goes black or void
    as though the keeper of the world
    has thrown the master switch.
The utter emptiness that is produced
    reverberates throughout my life
    and echoes back into the womb
    in sudden deja vu.

The part of me that's looking on
    knows mother is cut off by anesthesia
    and this is felt as death by fetus.
Intolerable separation,
    and in my life to come
    compulses me to rectify
    whenever love's withdrawn.

As I feel death
    I'm signaled by the hypnotist
    to be reborn,
    this time eliminating chemical intrusion.
And so, the smart of me that's looking on
    decides
    to lock the doctor in the closet.
Then with my mother's full attention
    I, fetus, slide out easily.

*In wonder*
        *through my new-born eyes,*
        *and through the eyes beneath my skin,*
        *I see a tiny, new-born hand—*
        *can even feel a perfect little hand.*
*I'm certain that a camera,*
        *if focused on the space adjoining wrist,*
        *would show on film*
        *an air-tight piece of evidence*
        *of crinkly, opalescent skin*
        *on tiny fingerbones.*

*I could have stayed an hour or more*
        *just savoring this new-born-ness.*
*But called by therapist*
        *to anchor and go on,*
        *I took the elevator up*
        *completing the experience.*

## Rattled

There is a trance induced by rattle—
      tradition used by shamans.
For this experience I place my body
      in prescribed position:
      I stand,
      feet parallel with knees unlocked,
      hands forming fists and placed
      with knuckles touching
      just above the navel,
      eyes closed
      and chin at slightly elevated angle.

The leader now begins
      to shake a rattle-gourd,
      the energy of rattle fitting rattler.
The sound of seeds
      inside this womb of gourd
      goes on for fifteen minutes,
      and I experience the following:

Slight tremors run their fingers
      up my spine;
      my jaw goes slack,
      unhinged somehow;
      I drool a little.
Then spasms,
      not seemingly controlled by me,
      take on my jaw and shake it.
I feel my jaw and teeth begin to grow;
      they soon seem strong enough
      to crush a skull
      or tear an antelope in two.

This weight of jaw then seems
      to rock me back and forth,
      and as I rock my feet begin to grow,
      develop claws that grip the earth
      allowing me to stand upright.
The warmth of fur creeps up my legs
      and over belly round and fat,
      then slowly covers arms.

It seems some eye inside can see
        this jaw, these claws, this fur,
        as clearly as I feel them.

Then jaw and feet and fur
        fall in upon themselves
        and settle in my shoulders
        which now feel powerful enough
        to bear my weight,
        invite some weight,
        to share it with my legs.

In all this time
        my mind does not come forth
        with words for my experience
        which stops when rattle stops.
The words come later.

The words come
        when the leader of the group conveys
        that certain clans believe
        this special kind of trance
        calls forth
        the Spirit of the Bear.

## Inner Messages

When I am in hypnotic trance,
  induced by others
  or by me,
  deliberately or otherwise
  some piece of information passes
  through my mouth
  into my brain
  so that I hear it as I say it,
  and wonder at my knowledge.

In meditative trance, however,
  my senses bear the messages:
  the words are felt
  and heard and smelled and tasted.
They come from vocal cords
  I know are not my own.

## Joining the Universal Oneness

In fantasy
   I climbed my favorite mountain top
   and there began my journey
   of going through, around,
   beyond the sky,
   to be the sky
   and hold the sun in lap,
   put out my tongue of energy
   to lick the planetary rainbows.

I traveled on
   to find the energy of sun,
   to enter it,
   to be the sunfire that transforms
   by bringing life to death
   and death to life
   so they are one.

And living now the energy of sunlife,
   I traveled through the barriers
   of time and space,
   formed liasons with all that was,
   and is,
   and evermore shall be.

I joined the here and now
   with timelessness and formlessness,
   lived in the energy of universal oneness,
   and still remained
   unique and separate.

## A Level Beyond

Good thing
this consciousness of mine has many levels.
It saved my life
the week I spent encapsuled with a shaman.

For level 2,
which I will call amenities,
was almost non-existent.
I wish that I could say the same for level 7,
which I call personality.
Now there was rank abundance!

However,
when I placed myself
beyond these surface levels
and found a higher stream of energy,
the voltage was empowering.

And there I rode the wings of God,
saw from afar the madness of the world
at levels 2 and 7.
Too distant were the sounds to reach my ears.
Too distant was the pettiness to touch my heart.

(2c) footnote

Some experiences seem so unusual and have such
power that shrines are built. But sometimes fears take
form and walls are built, instead of shrines, allowing
wonders to pass by unnoticed.

Such experiences often mark the sharp curves on
my path. "Message From Mother, October 19, 1985"
tells of an experience which took place just a few
hours before the poems of this trilogy began to flood
my life and cause a turning from which there was no
returning.

"Remembrance" is, in its own way, a footnote and
may shed light on Mother's message.

"Vision on a Mountain Road" was the experiential
seed that eventually blossomed into the willingness to
publish this poetry.

The other experiences and ceremonies in this sec-
tion took me around many bends and up steep hills
just as unusual experiences and ceremonies often do.

## Message from Mother
October 19, 1985

In class
a woman sits across from me.
I note she is a stranger.
Yet,
as I look I see my mother
who crossed over 20 years ago.
No matter how I turn my head
or blink my eyes,
or how the woman shifts position,
my mother's image remains clear.

At break
I take a close-up look and see
that only in a minor way
does she look like my mother.

I write all this in detail in my notes.
Perhaps I will find meaning.

Next morning as I meditate,
I try to wipe away the thoughts
and in that open space I hear a voice
or see a voice,
or smell a voice,
or feel it.
In all these ways I know it is my mother.

She speaks five words,
quite ordinary words.
She tells me,
"I will help you write."

And I believe she does.

## Remembrance

While pondering my fecundity,
    compared to former paucity,
    a curiosity arose
    of what my paucity consisted.

I could recall,
    in 60 years of writing very little,
    two pieces only that resembled poetry,
    both written 20 years ago.

The first described my pain in therapy.
The other was a poem of love
    delivered to my loved one
    the last time
    that I held her life-warmed hand
    on Mother's Day.

## Vision on a Mountain Road
### December 12, 1985

Today,
while driving in the sky
of snow-dust covered mountains,
a spirit arm reached out
and lifted me above myself.
And I looked down inside my head
to see a heavy door
that opened to a sunny place
which lit a book of poetry.

I knew
my poems were in this book,
and from the words inside
flowed streams of love and succor,
like life-lines of compassion.

I saw
the readers read the words
and feel
their own unspoken words were heard,
at last.

Then,
joy welled up and lifted me
to timeless space,
to meadows where my soul could graze
on tufts of purest colors.
'Til I,
now comforted by this brief visit home,
was gently lifted down
to join my earthling body,
which welcomed me with tears
along a road on snow-dust covered mountains.

## Night Vision

*This is the vision that I saw:*

*Each daughter born*
*was carried through a certain path*
*to birth herself.*

*I did not see the wings that carried her.*
*I only saw her struggling feet,*
*as very early in her life*
*her hand reached out*
*and drew her father up*
*to rest upon her back.*

*Together, then,*
*the two made passage through the mother—*
*much like a worm makes passage*
*through the earth—*
*ingesting energy from root to crown.*

*I saw in this transforming journey*
*each daughter builds a bridge*
*to father's isolation,*
*frees mother from the bonds of ownership,*
*and to herself*
*she gives the prize of wholeness,*
*much greater than the sum of parts.*

## Full Moon Ceremony
### May 23, 1986

I climbed the hill behind my house
  with energy thinned down by fasting.
I held a bloodstone in my hand
  and carried sage to purify.

On hilltop, then,
  I spread a rug to face the East
  and breathed a wreath of smoking sage.

Eyes closed,
  I called to spirits gone ahead
  from each of earth's directions.
And, as I did,
  an eye appeared behind my eyes.

From North an ancient eye of crone
  emerged from folds and folds of skin.
The eye of West was bold and male,
  unlike the eye of gentle maiden
  from the South.
But eye of East stabbed through my head
  much like a silver shooting star.

I called to transformation guide, Inanna,
  and many, many women's eyes,
  a stream of women's eyes,
  passed through my inward looking place.
Each eye was lit by different shades
  of green and blue,
  of lavender and pink and gold.

I had a sense of lifting up
  to meet a host of spirit guides,
  and as we met,
  I felt and tasted, smelled and saw
  the color blue.
Pervasively it filled my sensual universe.

Then, as the blue was lightened
   into lavender,
   some prayers for all the daughters
   of my lives
   blew through my lips like wisps of smoke
   that swirled and thickened into gray
   until my inner sky was black.

A far-off spot of light appeared
   as I felt sucked into a hole
   where glowing coal of single eye
   speared through my consciousness and pulled
   'til I exploded into whiteness.

Then brilliant fields of color
   pulsed my throat
   and filled me where no eyelid could protect
   from the intensity.
First came the reds and oranges,
   those strangers to my inner vision,
   then greens and blues,
   familiar friends.
But as the lavenders began to flow
   and pinks crept in,
   I knew I saw the color of my mother's soul
   and that all souls were passing in review,
   each robed in wondrous color.

Whoever lifted, lowered me,
   and bathed my cheeks with tears.
I felt that I had seen
   the secret of the universe.

## The Smell of Soul

In this temple I call body
    I have a place to smell out Soul.
It is the place of breathing my own breath.
It lies behind my eyes
    when they are blind with sight.
Tonight the smell is strong and sweet.

Routinely,
    I smell my juices sexual,
    my sweat, my body's residues—
    I taste the mucus of my nose, my tears,
    the flavors of my womanhood—
    I lick my skin.
All these are messages from self.

Tonight,
    I smell my Soul.
It has the smell of passage, change,
    of wisdom burnt,
    of womb,
    of ripening.
It has the smell of smokeless fire.
The hollows of my body fill with it.

My fingers stroke the golden chord.

## Sweat Lodge Ceremony

Deep in a night of air,
   so still all living things
   assume a stance of waiting,
   a moon, now on the lip of being full,
   shines out on rounds and rounds
   of small white puffs
   the spirits leave around
   when they are gathering.
The circle of the moon is circled, too,
   by rings of silver, gold, and amber;
   symbolic of our halos
   as we await our transformation ceremony
   through medium of sweat
   and prayers
   and white hot rocks.

For this,
   the earth presented 16 supple branches
   to form a double octagon of shelter.
The animals gave skins for roof,
   and ocean lined her shore with rocks
   for fire to purify.

Then,
   in the light from centered pit
   of glowing rocks
   we kneel on cedar boughs,
   presenting open hearts and minds,
   our bodies and our souls.

And here,
   through prayers and songs,
   and silences and sheddings,
   we're melted down to essence of our core
   that reaches through the earth
   and is the earth,
   and up through rings of moon
   into the distant space we fill
   as it fills us.

And we see God beneath our feet
   and in the stones
   and steam and sweat.
We see God in each other's faces.

*(3) footnote*

*My deepest beliefs and values help me to stand on solid ground in the quicksand of choices my world offers. Sometimes, when there are many ruts and boulders on my path my eyes become fixed and narrowed and I forget to gaze again at the beauty in variety, fearful of losing my footing. Then, in this fearfulness, I become immovable wrapped like a mummy in my principles. But, if I explore the territory with an open mind, mulch the ground of my convictions with possibilities, then I find nourishment for growth and am enriched. Come, explore with me the worlds of healing, spirit, and nature.*

*(3a) footnote*

*Trust love to heal*
*whatever form this love takes on.*
*The ways of healing are as countless as the stars.*
*Each kind of love connects us to the healing stream*
*and each provides the grace to open us for the receiving.*
*Trust love to heal*
*although its form may be a stranger.*

## Passion

Oh, treasure all your boiling passions—
    earthquakes of joy
    or lightning bolts of love;
    whirlwinds of hope,
    monsoons of tears,
    or fires of volcanic anger.

Oh, treasure all your boiling passions
    and feed them well.
They are the gifts you have
    for souls who dwell in other realms.
They are the coin of healing energy,
    the very stuff
    that holds the universe together.

So treasure all this juice your body spawns.
It is the key of life.

## Whose Blessing?

If I should use my eye
and look into your eye
to heal a part of you
that ruptured in the womb,
whose blessing will I have?

If I should take my healing hand
to stroke the golden cord
above your head
and open up your heart
to charismatic energy,
whose blessing will I have?

If I should take the smell of soul
while it is hot in me
and breathe it in some orifice
of yours
to fan your flame of creativity,
whose blessing will I have?

And if I place my crystal piece
upon a letter that you wrote in pain
and you are healed,
whose blessing will I have,
whose disbelief or apathy,
and whose disparagement?

Walk carefully with healing energy,
and place it well.
For witches have been burned,
and will again.

### Re-Creation

*"In the beginning God created..."*

*I think*
*creation is the separating out*
*of elements*
*to be combined in novel ways.*

*Yet, with one bite in Edenland*
*the secret of all unity was scattered.*
*An apple brought the curtain down*
*to seal the spot*
*where knowledge took the form of trees*
*and those who fled*
*snatched keys to be passed down*
*to chosen ones.*

*And such a one,*
*through memories or drums or potions,*
*can see the brokenness,*
*know where the missing pieces*
*can be found,*
*the formula to recombine.*

*Look to your prayers,*
*your dreams or meditations.*
*Perhaps a key has found its way*
*into your hand.*

## The Laying On of Hands

An upper room
    filled with the energy of eager hearts,
    of hungry hearts,
    of fearful, wounded hearts,
    each heart with hopes
    of melting down the fears
    and wounds and hungers,
    into a molten lovingness
    directed out through open hands
    to touch the hungry,
    longing ones
    stretched out and waiting
    for the blessings.

An upper room
    filled with the energy of open hearts
    of those who found
    a way to heal themselves,
    to feed themselves
    and calm their fears,
    by daring to reach out
    for energy from earth and sky
    and let it mingle
    with their blood and breath
    and freely flow
    to join the universal healing stream
    and touch with reverence the veil
    that hangs between the souls on earth,
    the veil we call the body.

Share in the energy of upper rooms.
You hold some magic in your hands,
    you feed it when you love yourself.
It multiplies when given.

## Medicine Woman Rites

Her syllables are few
  and sentences or paragraphs
  are luxuries she hoards.

She tunes the energy
  of whistles, drums, and rattles
  into a healing stream
  and focuses this energy of universe,
  like mirrors focus sun,
  until it burns
  to form a crystal core of clarity.
She lives this core,
  and through it sucks out evil.

She also gives her special kiss
  that bridges separation
  and in this reuniting, heals.

## The Healing Stream

You came to me.

I looked behind your masks
 and saw a sea of emptiness
 where love should be.

I offered up my fullness to your touch
 and gently touched your emptiness.

Together, in some place so deep
 it has no name,
 we found the color of a stream
 where nourishment exists
 for unborn love,
 the place where broken hearts
 are bathed.

Suffused in colors of this stream
 we talked of many things,
 made plans,
 shot laughter at the moon,
 held hands,
 marked progress on our calendars.

You even thought I was the source.
And you are lost now that I'm gone.

So come, sit quietly,
 until you find the color
 of the stream we found together;
 and place your heart and breath
 inside the stream,
 and feel again the love you felt for me,
 and see again my eye of love for you.

Then dare to make yourself the object
 of this mighty stream.
Immerse yourself and fall in love again.
You are the source.

## The Healer of Healers

Sweet Healer,
I know you and I love you.
I've walked with you,
    sat knee to knee with you
    in other times and other worlds.
You are my family.

Like you,
    my joy and sadness,
    anger, fear, and love,
    in tidal waves wash over me
    and help me see
    into the hiding place of sickness.

Like you,
    I've felt the searing pain
    of knives honed into being
    by the whetstone of initiation.
Like you,
    I've feared the skull of death,
    feared even more
    that I'd turn back
    and not break through the barrier
    towards healing.

I, too, suck with my hands
    and pull the enemy into the fires
    that flicker on my palms,
    then wave the ashes to the winds.

Dear Healer,
    sometimes at night,
    I feel your breath
    as you have come to me in dreams
    and other fantasies.
We've traveled roads
    that don't exist for others.
Our veins run red with mystery
    and secret doors appear
    in spots our feet have touched.

Some days, in sunlight,
    from my perch high on the rocks
    I see you lift your golden mane.
Sounds from our throats mate in the air.

74

*(3b) footnote*

*Once long ago, as I sat in my theater seat, the curtain parted and the newly released film "Doctor Zhivago" came on the screen. A winter graveyard scene appeared and then, four notes plucked by unseen fingers on the strings of a balalaika, pulled at a memory so dim, so ancient, and so powerful in me that my body seemed to melt away. Where did this memory come from? Where had I heard this sound before?*

*Sometimes, out of the corners of my eyes, I witness things too startling to believe. Yet, when I dare to share these experiences with others I often find I am not alone.*

## First Night of Life

*Sleep on sweet child*
  *and dream yourself into existence.*
*Your lids are closed*
  *against this world of unreality.*

*The mists*
  *from places you have been*
  *still cling to you.*
*But, dreaming thins them out*
  *and helps you gently bring yourself*
  *into this life to come.*

## Metamorphosis

*What does it mean to die so that I live?*

*That line dividing living death*
  *from death that lives*
  *is sometimes called illusion,*
  *the death of which brings life to life*
  *enabling me to see self,*
  *eye to eye.*

*It seems to me*
  *it is a letting go while holding on,*
  *relaxing hold so I fall free:*
  *finding the balance, infinitely delicate.*
*Some may achieve this state in trance*
  *and some through isolation.*

*However, I think*
  *tiny, insignificant events of everyday*
  *can hold the germ of dying that gives life,*
  *whenever love melts ego.*

## Old Souls

*Old souls*
*returned to life*
*have trouble being children.*

*The parents are confused by knowingness*
*wrapped in a child's body.*

*The children are confused by doubt*
*wrapped as a parent.*

## In Other Worlds

*So very old was I,*
*as wrinkled as last winter's apple,*
*liqueur of wisdom in my veins.*
*So very old was I,*
*dispensing potions.*

*And many came,*
*and they would come again*
*in different dress,*
*a hundred centuries later,*
*a tiny germ of memory*
*allowing glad reunion.*

## First Son

My son,
   who is the sun,
   brings warmth and joy
   into my life,
   explores the earth,
   walks in the paths we walked
   in other lives,
   brings back to me
   some token
   from those long-forgotten places.

Dear son,
   our natures have a close relationship.
We can embrace without abrasion,
   your melody in harmony with mine.

How rarely
   is a gift like this bestowed,
   how rarely
   tasted on a conscious level,
   how rarely
   thanked.

My son,
   who was and ever is
   a joy to me.

## To Daughters Found Along the Way

I do believe
    the master plan of life dictates
    that we select our parents
    in order to work out the wrinkles
    of our former lives.
I trust that you selected well.

I don't know how your mother feels,
    if she appreciates
    the lovely creature that you are.

I'm glad I found you when I did.
And, if I have that choice
    next time around,
    I'd like to spend a lifetime
    in relationship with you.

## Life Cycles:
### Happy Birth and Death Days

My births are like a faucet's drippings,
each droplet is a global universe:
Released from eye of womb,
in falling, takes the form of tears.

Where did this stream of births begin?
Where does the wind begin?
Or where begins the tide?

The eons of the universe of time are named,
as though in naming we can find beginnings.
And, myths are made
as though by stretching circles
lines will form,
as though a hammer held aloft
can pound a nail into a spot called birth,
and following that line
can mark a cross at death...

I think that nail and cross are one,
and hammer sounds
are just collected breaths of universe,
and change is in the falling
and in the merging with the stream;
and forming, falling, merging, dying
are merely turnings of the eye of Oneness.

## In the Beginning

Then—
in my dim and ancient past
beyond recall,
when I could talk with animals
and change my skin,
just as the snake,
instead of dying—
I felt no pain.
For pain comes from the stiffening
with no release.

And in this dim and ancient past
beyond recall
the earth and sky,
from time to time,
exchanged their places in the sun.
And so we creatures learned to walk
and swim and fly.

Then, all the tears and oceans were as one,
nor was the breathing separate
from the winds,
nor anger from the fire,
nor joy from sun and moon
and constellations.

Oh, how I long
for dim and ancient past beyond recall,
and mourn the separations that exist.
Where is the oil
to soften all the stiffening
so I may shed myself again?

## Invocation

*Shake me awake from dreams.*
*Rattle my bones.*
*Drum on my soul.*
*Burn off my doubt.*
*Spirit of a living God*
*fall fresh on me.*

*(3c) footnote*

*Many of us talk to beings whom we cannot see. We call them saints or spirit guides, angels, God. We call our conversations prayers or reveries, communings with a loved one on the other side. If we look softly as we talk, our earthly eyes may even find the world of spirit living everywhere.*

## What Is the Address of Your Soul?

No microscope has brought one into focus.
No telescope has found one in the sky.
Exploratory surgery
        comes up with empty probe.
If one is pressed
        between the pages of some holy book,
        no earthquake ever shook it out.

Mathematical equations come and go
        yet none has had its name.
No clapper of the steeple bells
        has hit its note,
        nor chimney sweeps nor witches brooms
        picked up its trail.

Yet, take a poll on any busy corner
        and most will say they have one.

## Guardian Angels

Newborn,
  you brought along your spirit guides.
They drift around your bed at night,
  caress the arms that rock you,
  provide a channel for the flow of love.

Newborn,
  your spirit guides, like elves,
  peep out from all the creases of your soul,
  sometimes wave playfully,
  as though they orchestrate the smiles
  of joy and tenderness
  from those who hold you heart to heart.

Newborn,
  these spirit guides direct your eyes
  past all the masks and shells
  into the secret space of hearts,
  and help you speak to them
  in truths no words can match for purity.

And as I gaze and cradle you,
  the spirits of the old and new
  commune again,
  renewing old, enriching new.

## Generation Gap

When I burned sage
    on Mother's grave,
    the smoke curled in
    and touched her funny bone,
    so far removed this ritual
    from any that she ever practiced.

When I threw ashes
    from the sage to feed the earth,
    I felt the tickling of her toes,
    and saw again
    the callused knees
    that twinned her cleanliness with God.

I think my mother's learned a thing or two
    in other realms.
To show her pleasure in my ritual,
    she shone the color of her soul
    upon the marble slab
    that held the burning sage.

## Intense-City

Such density
intensity lays down in cities,
each layer breeding more,
and leaching playfulness from bodies.

The stabs of light
that try to pierce the darkness there
are blunted
from the grasping hands,
from love frowned into dogma,
from fire that stays in arms
stretched out for power and riches.

The smoke from daily prayers
is weighted down with asking.
It rises weakly,
seeking cracks
in all the walls of wanting,
and tries to find the healing streams
of thankfulness and self-forgiveness.

Where is the good news
that can thin this density?
When will the lightening occur
to clear the film from eyes
straining to see the unseen entities
with messages from other worlds?

The when and where
are held in hands and hearts
of loving souls
whose breathing lightens density
of the intensity in cities.

The universe has placed these blessed few,
like lightning bugs,
to scatter sparks of love
until a beacon forms
to shine into the eyes of God.

## The Soul of Alexa

Chameleon that you are,
   now camouflaged in baby skin,
   I see you looking
   through the midnight blue
   of infant eyes
   that shade you from detection.

I only know for certain you exist
   in moments when you've gone
   exploring other worlds,
   leaving Alexa thinly wrapped
   in personality of three weeks old.

## Message from the Other Side

Do spirits,
    once released from chosen incarnations,
    remain in trees they planted
    in some lifetime,
    and can we climb to get a blessing
    in the swaying branches?

I asked myself,
    if I go back to see the trees
    of father's childhood
    and trees that guard his grave,
    will his wings fan the leaves
    to welcome me?

To find my answer
    I went back, and saw instead,
    a message he had left for me
    in wisps of breeze
    that drew my eye to far horizons.

The message said,
    "Come,
    soar,
    reach high,
    go far—
    touch all or any tree on earth
    and you touch me
    and I touch you."

## Chicago Evening

A cat, a mask,
four women in an upper room
surrounded by cracked-open fairytales,
their own,
and those scooped high into a mountain
called Chicago.

As to the cat,
unseen by all except the mask,
its history was recounted,
and all the sightings of it.

As to the mask,
it has a written history,
authenticated by the Customs' stamp,
born of black fingers
mating leopard skin and cowrie shells,
survivor of some holocausts,
one known to present company—
the cat may know of others.

As to the four,
what shall I say?
It seems that one of them provided warp
while three took strands of memories
they'd kept as fairytales,
and in the weaving
found realities
that fired up back burners of their lives
and opened windows stuck by doubt.

And when the clock began to tick again,
four lightened hearts held hands
and saw a magic carpet
had been woven from the sharings;
and riding it—
a cat
and mask.

## Witch Hunt

The burning of my body at the stake
   lit up the sky
   just as my work brought light to earth.

No different was the smell
   of burning flesh to me
   than full moon boiling energy.

The only torture of my burning at the stake
   was waiting for the spark to catch,
   for in the flames
   were goddesses and mothers
   who gathered at my feet
   to guide me through the transformation.

Their fingers closed my eyelids
   to the jeering crowd
   and stroked my flesh
   to form the ash.
Their dancing wings and songs of joy
   released my soul
   to ride my ashes on the wind
   toward heaven.

I tell you this
   so when you honor me
   you'll celebrate the fiery ladder as a gift,
   rejoice with me that I was chosen.

## My Spirit Guide of Life

With shaman's drumbeat in the air,
    my breath, my blood, my body
    opened to a knowingness of lifetime presence
    felt beneath the surface of my consciousness,
    now rising to the top
    stirred up by beating drum.

When I called for a name from spirit guide,
    she answered back, "Diana."
Then, in the space of time that takes no time
    yet draws out endlessly,
    she told in thoughts that have no words
    the purpose and significance of womanhood
    for me and women everywhere.

When drumbeat stopped
    Diana, too, fell silent.
But as a sign that womanhood had come of age
    she left behind her palm print on my shoulder.

*(3d) footnote*

*God carves our lessons on the wind*
*and whispers them to rocks.*
*And if we listen to the rocks*
*or touch the wind*
*or catch the tears from fallen trees,*
*we'll fill the stomachs of our souls*
*with nourishment from nature.*

## Purification

*Lean on a tree*
*or wrap your arms around it.*
*Choose one whose girth exceeds your span,*
*for it has roots that travel to the core,*
*feed from the source.*

*Lean on a tree*
*to pass on negativity you brew yourself*
*or pick up from another . . .*
*for trees return all negativity*
*into the earth to purify.*

## Another Reality

I think that flowers
   bloom beneath my skin,
   and wind rides through my veins
   on harnessed cells.
Sometimes the sky plays peek-a-boo
   inside my head
   and heart beats clouds of different size.

I think a world of birds flies in my ears,
   cool air from feathers
   stills my brain in sleep;
   and trees of various shapes and flexibility,
   sometimes confused with bones and cartilage,
   run up my legs.

On many days
   I live and move and have my being
   in ignorance of all of this.

## Big Sur

*I love*
*those blessed, silent cliffs*
*with jaws set firm*
*against the sky and water,*
*with foam licked lips*
*and eagle feathers on their brows.*

*I lift my head*
*and in the roar from wind and wave*
*and lions of the sea,*
*the thunder of their silence reigns.*
*My heart is stilled to whisperings.*

## High Sierras

I saw the giant pebbles
   set by the gods
   to form the granite castles.
I saw the gouges
   that their fingers made
   to pool their tears,
   the eyes they placed in domes
   to guard their playgrounds
   when their elders called them home.

In silences they left behind,
   their frozen spit tore towers
   from the castles
   and split the granite moats.
The glaciers,
   mating with the pools of tears,
   spawned emerald lakes.

I walked this playground of the gods
   and saw all creatures move with grace
   because those eyes
   set in the rocks
   still watch,
   and guard,
   and smile.

## Giants of the Earth

I pressed my forehead
    to the mossy bark of redwood
    and felt my prayers drawn up
    and blown towards heaven.

I laid my cheek
    against the wrinkled skin of redwood
    and felt my cares melt into roots
    cupping the center of the earth.

I pressed my lips
    to ancient scars of redwood
    and kissed the blessed strength
    formed by the thousand rings.

I placed my ear
    deep in the furrows of the redwood
    and listened for the messages
    it gathered from the wind.

I longed to hear my name,
    and in that sound
    be re-united with the redwood.

## Atlantis

A time,
 a state of mind,
 a continent,
 where all the veils that separate
 are lifted by the shifting light
 reflected in the waters.

A time,
 a state of mind,
 a continent,
 where feelings manifest in colors,
 or drift as fragrances,
 or take the form of notes
 played on exotic instruments;
 sometimes collecting into oceans,
 or in bodies
 that enfold the people.

A time,
 a state of mind,
 a continent;
 where skin and flesh
 slide in between the molecules of rocks
 or trees or anything
 that welcomes them;
 where opening and closing are the same,
 and being home is everywhere,
 and everyone,
 and ecstacy is in the flow
 of joining and rejoining
 without the need to separate;
 where looking at the wild elephant
 is just the same as living in its skin,
 and smelling creatures of the sea
 provides the gills for breathing.

The secret of this state of mind
 or continent with interchanging parts
 is in the balancing,
 and as the story goes,
 to keep the secret of the balance safe
 the ones who ruled locked it away.

And so Atlantis tipped and fell into the sea.

## White Elk

*Your horns are white,*
*and white bleeds through the layers*
*of your soul.*
*Your bones*
*are testaments,*
*collecting in the earth,*
*that strength exists in many forms.*

## Mount Shasta

Queen Shasta
  wears a robe of white
  and diamonds live
  on all the fingers of her hair.
Her beauty charms the spirit world
  and from the seven seas
  she draws the ones who lost their footing
  when Atlantis sank.

Today,
  I picnicked on her slope
  and felt a pull to join the spirits
  on her breasts.
I smelled the marbled salt
  that washed her feet in other times,
  and saw the gash of avalanche
  made by her belly laughs.

Queen Shasta
  wears a robe of white.
She is a siren of the sky
  who beckons to the spirits passing by.
But we,
  who are embodied still,
  stand back in awe
  and long to hear her call.

### Pacific Lumber Company
### Redwood Sawmill
### Scotia, California

I saw a slaughterhouse of giants,
    their limbs left rotting in the forest.
I saw them skinned in scalding baths,
    their trunks cut through by steel.

My tears for them were blown away
    with dust from saws
    that sliced these giants into forms
    transferring shelter
    from the creatures of the air
    to us who walk on earth.

So sprinkle corn upon the doorway
    of your house
    and thank the giants
    slaughtered for your warmth,
    and bless their sacrifice.

## The Disappearance of the Anasazi
## From Canyon de Chelly

Which sliver of a moon
      tipped down to scoop you up?
Which darkened sun removed you,
      shadow first?
Where are you hiding
      the remains of bodies that you shed
      while leaving skeletons of dwellings
      on display?

Last night I saw the ghosts of you
      that cover Spider Mountain,
      no number large enough
      to take your count.
I smelled the residue you left behind
      for dawn to burn away.

Is there some lesson for us
      in your disappearance?
Are mysteries placed in this world
      to teach?
Perhaps they are
      like open-ended questions
      with strings attached to draw us out,
      expand our realm of possibilities,
      increase our ponderings,
      build breezeways for our little minds
      that so prefer an airtight case.

## On Mountain Path

*I met a man*
    *while walking on a mountain path.*
*His face was bare of masks.*
*His wrinkles smooth with love.*
*His soul smiled*
    *in the corners of his mouth.*
*His eyes were innocent—*
    *yet wise.*

*I felt a blessing from his look,*
    *and hoped his heart was one*
    *that tunes the universe.*

## Twilight Yearning

The wind dies down
and signals for a silent space
at twilight.

My heart dies down
and signals toward an empty place
at twilight.

In silent space
I long to hold the sun up from its setting.
In empty place
I long to hold my heart up from its sinking.

At twilight
when the wind dies down
and creatures hold their breath,
the birds join wings
to let the rising warmth of earth
lift them towards home.

I listen to the silence
in the empty place
and look for rising warmth
to carry me towards home,
at twilight.

# To Help You Find Your Favorite Poems

**110**